Fletcher,
Hope you enjoy ...
birds are so fun.

J...

BABY BIRDS

Rio Nuevo Publishers®
P.O. Box 5250, Tucson, Arizona 85703-0250
(520) 623-9558, www.rionuevo.com

Design: Karen Schober, Seattle, Washington

Front cover: white tern chick; back cover: least terns; page 1: white tern; pages 2–3:
Pacific loons.

Library of Congress Cataloging-in-Publication Data

Rich, Jeffrey.
Baby birds / Jeffrey Rich.
     p. cm. -- (Look west series)
ISBN-13: 978-1-887896-70-2 (hardcover)
ISBN-10: 1-887896-70-8 (hardcover)
1. Birds. 2. Birds--Infancy. I. Title. II. Series: Look West.
QL673.R53 2005
598.13'9--dc22
                              2005009647
Printed in Hong Kong
10 9 8 7 6 5 4 3 2 1

BABY BIRDS

Jeffrey Rich

RIO NUEVO PUBLISHERS
TUCSON, ARIZONA

WATCHING A BABY BIRD HATCH FROM ITS
EGG IS TO WITNESS ONE OF THE TRUE MIRACLES OF
LIFE, AND PHOTOGRAPHING THAT MIRACLE IS MY PASSION.
AT FIRST THERE IS A SMALL CRACK, THEN A SMALL HOLE,
AND THEN, IN A FEW MORE MOMENTS, THE EGG TOOTH
APPEARS—A HARDENED AREA ON TOP OF BABY BEAKS THAT
HELPS CRACK THE EGG OPEN FOR HATCHING. THE EGG
TOOTH WILL DISAPPEAR A FEW DAYS AFTER THE
CHICK IS OUT IN THE WORLD.

As a wildlife photographer, I often have to lie on the ground to get eye-to-eye with the nests, and frequently get my shots from behind a blind. I know that no photo is worth disturbing or harming the animal in any way. So setting up a blind helps to eliminate stress and

LEFT: *Newly hatched American avocet.* ABOVE: *Arctic terns.*

allows the subjects to go about their normal lives. My favorite hiding place is a floating blind, which allows me to position my camera only inches above the water line as my legs dangle under me.

Northern rough-legged hawk with a vole in its mouth for the chicks.

Aside from taking photos, I have had other opportunities to work with birds, including helping out at hack sites—artificial nests where baby birds hatched in captivity are released into the wild. These sites have been effective tools for increasing raptor populations such as eagles, falcons, and the now-famous California condor.

Hatchlings fall into two main developmental groupings. Baby birds born helpless and naked in the nest are considered "altricial." These young rely on their parents for everything. The adults feed them, keep them warm, keep them safe from predators, carry their waste away from the nest, and give the chicks anything else they might need. Sound familiar?

"Precocial" babies, on the other hand, possess many qualities that help them survive with less parental support. A precocial chick can walk and often run within minutes of hatching. They find their own food, come well camouflaged, and know how to hide soon after hatching. Parents brood their precocial chicks for warmth, and the adults often steer predators away. Different subgroupings occur within altricial and precocial, as different species exhibit varying degrees of development.

For most species, nesting generally takes place in summer. Some species may nest more than once in the same season. Some birds, if their nest is destroyed, will lay a new clutch of eggs, called double clutching.

Most birds don't nest during winter but migrate to areas with ample food and better weather.

Feathers are an amazing adaptation that makes birds unique. Feathers allow birds to fly, keep them warm, and act as camouflage. Bright and colorful feathers also function as attractions for breeding. But above all, feathers don't weigh very much. Lightweight feathers and hollow bones, combined with huge breast muscles attached to a wish bone (furcula), are what give birds the needed adaptations for flight.

Many birds show sexual dimorphism, meaning the male and female look different. Often the male's feathers are more colorful than the female's. In some species the male may be larger; in others the females are larger. Yet there are also many species where male and female look very similar, without any obvious differences.

ORDERS IN THE BIRD WORLD

Taking my cue from birding field guides, I have organized this book in phylogenetic order—that is, with the oldest species first. The birds related to the most ancient bird fossils appear at the front of the book, with the more recent arrivals, belonging to the Passerine order, at the end of the book.

Considered the two oldest living orders of birds, the **loons** (**Gaviiformes**) and **grebes** (**Podicipediformes**) are exceptionally good divers. They hunt for fish by diving underwater and swimming after them. Their feet are placed way back on the body, which allows them to swim quite well.

Albatross fall into the **seabird** order (**Procellariiformes**) and are often called "tube noses" because of an adaptation that allows the salt from ocean water to be expelled. On their beaks you will notice a long tube emptying to a groove that extends to the tip of the beak. The **Pelecaniformes** order includes **tropicbirds** and **cormorants,** which are related to **pelicans** and **boobies.** This diverse group of seabirds and waterbirds are unique in many ways.

Herons and **egrets** fall under the **Ciconiiformes** order, long-legged wading birds with long, pointed beaks. Many species in

Laysan albatross chick.

Tundra swan cygnet.

this group used to be hunted for their breeding feathers—beautiful plumes used for hats and other adornments. Because of this, their numbers declined in the early 1900s. **Waterfowl** (the order **Anseriformes**) include ducks, geese, and swans, the great swimmers and water lovers of the bird world. Most waterfowl species lay eggs that all hatch about the same time, because incubation doesn't begin until all the eggs are in the nest. This synchronous hatching is very common among precocial young.

Raptors, the hunters or birds of prey (**Falconiformes**), have sharp beaks and talons for catching and eating meat. Asynchronous hatching is characteristic of raptor nesting, with one egg laid each day or two, and incubation starting as soon as the first one is laid. This way, a "clutch" of five eggs could hatch over a ten-day period, creating a size difference in the young. The older, more developed chicks can out-compete their younger, weaker siblings for food and have been known to knock the younger ones out of the nest to their deaths.

Cranes, coots, and **rails** (in the order **Gruiformes**) fly with their necks out and feet trailing behind. They spend most of their lives in the air or on the ground, usually near water. This group includes the heaviest and tallest flying birds.

Shorebirds are aptly named for their habitat. They often have long bills to probe the exposed mudflats and shorelines for invertebrates such as polychaete worms, crustaceans, mollusks, and insects. Along with **gulls** and **terns,** shorebirds make up the order **Charadriiformes**. Different kinds of shorebirds can share the same territory because their specialized beaks allow them to feed side by side. Each unique bill captures a different type of prey, so they don't directly compete with each other for food. Amazing fliers and fish

Western grebe with newborn on its back.

hunters, terns will hover above, then dive into the water after their prey. "Seagull" is actually a misnomer; the correct term is gull. Gulls don't live at sea but are linked to it by their seashore existence. Many species of gulls will also live inland and find the shoreline habitat of lakes and waterways adequate for survival.

Owls (in the order **Strigiformes**) are famous for their sense of sight, especially night vision. Owls have huge eyes for their body size; human eyes would have to be the size of tennis balls by comparison. Hooters' eyes have an abundance of rods. Rods and cones are the cells that allow eyeballs to gather light and see in color. Having all these rods gives owls great night vision, whereas all the cones in human eyes allow us a greater rainbow of colors. The feathers around owls' eyes make up the facial disk, which is shaped like a satellite dish—perfect for gathering sound waves. Owls can hunt by sound as well as sight, a combination that makes them incredible predators.

Great horned owl chick.

Hummingbirds, the jewels of flight, are related to swifts (in the **Apodiformes** order). Hummers, as birders call them, are fascinating creatures whose flying abilities make the Wright Brothers look like rookies. With over three hundred species in the world, only sixteen nest in North America. These smallest of all birds have amazing metabolisms that allow their wings to beat over sixty times per second, with a heart rate of over two hundred beats per minute.

Flickers are members of the **woodpecker** order (**Piciformes**). These birds are well known for hollowing out trees and using the holes as nesting cavities. The following year they will make a new nest, and last year's nest often gets used by secondary cavity nesters such as bluebirds and kestrels.

Perching birds, in the **Passeriformes** order, are commonly referred to as passerines. This group contains the most birds and many different varieties, including robins, bluebirds, blackbirds, sparrows, warblers, and finches. A ligament in the passerine leg and foot causes the toes to close tightly around a perch when their legs bend. As the bird stands back up, the ligament loosens its grip and the toes release and open. This is how passerines can stay on a branch when they are sleeping or just relaxing.

PACIFIC LOON ✣ *GAVIA PACIFICA*

DIVING PREDATORS.

Loons are so well known for their beautiful and haunting calls that we often hear them in the movies, making the loon a Hollywood bird. If you ever get the chance to hear this magical call, you will remember it forever. The only time loons come to land is for nesting, always on the ground near a freshwater shoreline.

HABITAT coastal in winter; nests near fresh water

RANGE Pacific coast of North America in winter; northern Canada and Alaska for summer

ORDER Gaviiformes: the loons

YOUNG precocial

CLUTCH SIZE 2

Pacific loon.

EARED GREBE ✠ *PODICEPS NIGRICOLLIS*
WESTERN GREBE ✠ *AECHMOPHORUS OCCIDENTALIS*
CLARK'S GREBE ✠ *AECHMOPHORUS CLARKII*

PIGGYBACK RIDERS.

Western grebes and Clark's grebes, once considered a single species, are now separated into two, although they retain very similar appearances and behaviors. The eared grebe also shares one especially interesting behavior of the grebe family: When the young hatch they leave the egg and head up onto the mother's back. The parent

Clark's grebes.

even puts its foot out as a step to help the baby get a boost up. Once the chick reaches the parent's back it will actually "disappear" under the feathers—a very safe spot for the young, who will stay there for the first few days of life. Grebes even eat feathers, and some of the babies' first meals are feathers. One theory suggests the feathers line the digestive tract to protect from the sharp bones and scales in the grebes' fishy diet. All three types of grebes construct their nests of floating mats of vegetation.

HABITAT along lakes, wetlands, and seacoasts (both fresh and salt water); winters near coastlines from Washington to Louisiana
RANGE winters along U.S. west coast (eared grebe range extends to Louisiana); nests inland to mid-continent
ORDER Podicipediformes: the grebes
YOUNG subprecocial
CLUTCH SIZE 3–4

LAYSAN ALBATROSS *PHOEBASTRIA IMMUTABILIS*
BLACK-FOOTED ALBATROSS *PHOEBASTRIA NIGRIPES*
GOONEY BIRDS.

One of my most memorable bird observations was watching albatross, also called gooney birds, doing their mating dance and caring for their chicks. Mating season starts with an intricate display of bowing, rubbing beaks, and making cooing noises. They produce one egg, then share the incubation duties. Once the chick hatches, the remarkable job of feeding begins. The adults will fly out to sea, often over a thousand miles, in search of food. Some adults will fly to Alaskan waters to find food for their chicks back on Midway Island in the middle of the Pacific Ocean. When they come back

Laysan albatross.

days later, it is amazing they can find their chicks, as the island is literally covered with nests and babies.

HABITAT open ocean, except when ground-nesting in Hawaiian Islands and Midway
RANGE Pacific Ocean
ORDER Procellariiformes: the tube noses
YOUNG semialtricial
CLUTCH SIZE 1

RED-TAILED TROPICBIRD ⚐ *PHAETHON RUBRICAUDA*

PACIFIC ISLANDERS WITH FLASHING RED STREAMERS.

A beautiful white bird with an extremely long red tail consisting of only two feathers. The mother lays one egg on the ground near protective vegetation. Watching these spectacular fliers in flight with the long trailing tail is truly a birding sight. Unlike ocean birds such as puffins and auks that swim better than they fly, many seabirds spend a great deal of their lives gliding over the open ocean, coming to land only for nesting.

HABITAT open ocean, except when nesting on ground near vegetation of remote oceanic islands

RANGE tropical and subtropical Pacific Ocean

ORDER Pelecaniformes: web-footed swimmers

YOUNG semialtricial

CLUTCH SIZE 1

Adult red-tailed tropicbird.

DOUBLE-CRESTED CORMORANT ⤳ *PHALACROCORAX AURITUS*

TIME TO ADD MORE OIL.

These great swimmers and divers eat fish and can go as deep as one hundred feet to capture their prey. Since their feathers are not naturally waterproof they must come out of the water and dry their wings, unlike most other diving birds. Once out of the water they will sit with their wings open to dry. With their dark bodies absorbing the heat of the sunshine, they look like bird mannequins in that classic cormorant pose. They also use oil from the uropygial gland at the base of the tail to spread over their feathers, which provides some water-resistance. They build stick nests and often nest communally.

Double-crested cormorant.

HABITAT wetlands, coasts, lakes, and rivers
RANGE common throughout the U.S.
ORDER Pelecaniformes: web-footed swimmers
YOUNG altricial
CLUTCH SIZE 3–4

SNOWY EGRET ⊰ *EGRETTA THULA*

IT TAKES A VILLAGE TO RAISE A SNOWY EGRET.

Cousins to the herons, egrets hunt fish, amphibians, and aquatic invertebrates in shallow water. The snowy egret will stand motionless, peering into the water, and upon spotting its prey will lunge headfirst and seize it in the long, sharp bill. Once the critter is caught the heron has to position it headfirst for swallowing whole. This often involves tossing the prey up in the air to re-catch it at a better angle. Then you can see the large bulge traveling down the bird's long neck.

HABITAT wetlands, nesting colonially in trees and shrubs

RANGE coastal areas from Oregon south, Texas to Florida and up the East Coast; some nest more inland, east to Colorado and north to Oklahoma

ORDER Ciconiiformes: the herons and egrets

YOUNG altricial

CLUTCH SIZE 3–4

ABOVE: *Snowy egret fledgling, preening.*
RIGHT: *Begging mother for food.*

TRUMPETER SWAN ≼ *CYGNUS BUCCINATOR*
TUNDRA SWAN ≼ *CYGNUS COLUMBIANUS*
LARGEST WATERFOWL IN THE WORLD.

Aside from size and bill coloration, these two North American swans look a lot alike. Trumpeters—the largest waterfowl native to North America—weigh twenty to thirty pounds, with a wingspan of about seven feet. Trumpeters are found mostly in the northern Rocky Mountain states and are on the endangered species list. They will often nest along the Madison River in Yellowstone National Park in Wyoming. Tundra swans aren't endangered and nest in the Arctic, wintering in the northern coastal areas of the lower forty-eight states. Newly hatched, down-covered cygnets look like little floating "puffballs."

HABITAT freshwater wetlands (marshes, ponds, lakes, estuaries), nesting on ground near water
RANGE trumpeter: scattered

Trumpeter swans.

throughout Nebraska, Wyoming, Montana, Nevada, Oregon, Washington, and north into Alaska; tundra: winters in flocks along both U.S. coasts and as far inland as Utah

ORDER Anseriformes: the waterfowl

YOUNG precocial

CLUTCH SIZE trumpeters 3–9, tundras 3–5

CANADA GOOSE ⤙ *BRANTA CANADENSIS*

THEY HONK IN THE WILDERNESS, NOT ON THE HIGHWAY.

One of the most common waterfowl is the Canada goose. In some places the goose population has become problematic. These areas include urban lakeshores, parks, golf courses, and lawns, where we have created a perfect habitat for the goose, with an ample food supply and no predators. Some geese will nest and actually attack people while defending their families. Their droppings create a mess in these park-like areas too. The Canada goose—a favorite of hunters—is a perfect example of a hunted species that still thrives in our human-dominated landscape. Their characteristic honking call is recognized by most people and gives us a sense of wildness right in our own back yards.

HABITAT freshwater wetlands (marshes, ponds, lakes, estuaries), nesting on islands and near water

RANGE throughout North America

ORDER Anseriformes: the waterfowl

YOUNG precocial

CLUTCH SIZE 4–6

Canada geese.

MALLARD ᐳ *ANAS PLATYRHYNCHOS*
WOOD DUCK ᐳ *AIX SPONSA*

LET'S PLAY FOLLOW THE LEADER!

Ducks, related to swans and geese, are the smallest of the waterfowl. Ducks are famous for "imprinting"—an adaptation wherein a newborn will follow the first thing it sees. Even a group of fifteen young ducklings will stay close together, all swimming around mom, actively feeding—a per-

Mallard chick.

fect form of protection. Mallards—with the male's characteristic green head—are the best-known ducks in the U.S. Wildlife biologists are responsible for bringing the wood duck—one of North America's most colorful birds—back from near extinction. In the early 1900s there were very few of them, due to over-hunting and loss of habitat. With laws put in place to protect them and with improvements in their nesting habitat, they are now doing well.

Wood ducks nest in cavities in old trees and snags and will use man-made nest boxes too. Unlike swans and geese, ducks exhibit sexual dimorphism, with males more colorful than females.

Wood ducks.

HABITAT mallard: wetlands, ground-nesting near water; wood ducks: open woodlands near water, wetlands with woody vegetative cover, nesting in cavities and nest boxes

RANGE throughout North America (wood ducks not found in the Southwest)

ORDER Anseriformes: the waterfowl

YOUNG precocial

CLUTCH SIZE 6–15

ROUGH-LEGGED HAWK ≼ *BUTEO LAGOPUS*
RED-TAILED HAWK ≼ *BUTEO JAMAICENSIS*

HIGH-SOARING HUNTERS.

In the asynchronous nest of this rough-legged hawk were five eggs, so the first baby hatched at least five days ahead of the last one. This red-tailed hawk is already out of the nest and learning how to fly, with two siblings nearby. The red-tailed, our most common hawk, is the only one with a reddish tail, making identification easy in adult birds. When baby birds leave the nest they are called fledglings. When altricial chicks first fly out of the nest the parents will continue to bring them food until they learn to hunt on their own.

HABITAT rough-legged: open country and marshes in winter, summer in the Arctic; red-tailed: many diverse habitats from deserts to coastal areas; simple nests on ground or cliffs RANGE rough-legged: nests in Arctic and winters in all but southernmost of the lower 48 states; red-tailed: throughout North America ORDER Falconiformes: the raptors

Fledgling red-tailed hawk.

Rough-legged hawk chicks.

YOUNG semialtricial, asynchronous

CLUTCH SIZE rough-legged 2–7, red-tailed 1–3

NORTHERN HARRIER ⌐ *CIRCUS CYANEUS*
AEROBATIC CIRCUS FLIER.

Formerly called the marsh hawk, a few years ago it became the northern harrier. Renaming is common in the ornithology world as new information comes to light about certain species. Harriers are among the most agile and acrobatic raptors in North America. While hunting, the harrier will fly very low to the ground, soaring with wings slightly upturned in a V shape. Harriers use their hearing to locate rodents, birds, and frogs in the grassy land below. If you look closely you will notice the adults have a facial disk much like an owl's.

Northern harrier nest with chick and eggs.

HABITAT wetlands and open fields; nests on ground or over water on platform of vegetation such as cattails

RANGE throughout North America

ORDER Falconiformes: the raptors

YOUNG semialtricial, asynchronous

CLUTCH SIZE 4–6

BALD EAGLE ⟅ *HALIAEETUS LEUCOCEPHALUS*

OUR NATIONAL SYMBOL.

Our country's symbol, the bald eagle, is a regal bird with white head and tail, although juveniles are brownish overall. It takes four to five years to attain the adult coloration. While in the nest the chicks

have huge feet and beaks for their size and eventually grow into them. These are very helpful in holding and eating the meat that the adults bring to the nest. When raptors fledge, they are full grown and often heavier than the parents. Recently downlisted from endangered to threatened status, our national bird has become a great comeback story for wildlife conservation.

HABITAT near water, nesting in tall trees or cliffs; will add sticks to nest annually (one nest was found weighing over two tons)

RANGE throughout North America, more in Canada and Alaska

ORDER Falconiformes: the raptors

YOUNG semialtricial, asynchronous

CLUTCH SIZE 1–3

LEFT AND ABOVE: *Bald eagle in nest with chicks.*

PRAIRIE FALCON ⊰ *FALCO MEXICANUS*
AMERICAN KESTREL ⊰ *FALCO SPARVERIUS*
FLYING, SWOOPING, DIVE-BOMBING HUNTERS.

Prairie falcon.

Prairie falcons range throughout the West and prefer open areas (such as prairies). These fast fliers will prey on birds and small mammals, diving in at high speeds to capture a meal. American kestrels, on the other hand, will watch from a perch for prey and then hover in flight before diving on dinner—usually small mammals, insects, and reptiles. North America's smallest, most colorful, and most commonly seen falcon, the American kestrel will nest in secondary cavities and also uses manmade nest boxes. Most birds of prey are sexually dimorphic in size, with females larger than males. In the case of the kestrel, however, the sexual differences also include color, as the male has blue on the wings.

HABITAT prairie falcon: dry open country and prairies, nesting on cliffs; American kestrel: open country and near cities

RANGE prairie falcon: western U.S.; American kestrel: throughout North America

ORDER Falconiformes: the raptors

YOUNG semialtricial, asynchronous

CLUTCH SIZE 3–5

American kestrel fledgling on its nest box.

OSPREY ⊰ *PANDION HALIAETUS*

FISHERMAN EXTRAORDINAIRE.

A rather specialized raptor, the osprey is an expert fisherman. They will dive down into the water feet first, hitting the fish with their amazing talons. Their two outer toes can be reversed so two toes point forward and two backward (zygodactyl), which gives a tight grasp on the fish. They also have "spicules" on the bottoms of their feet. These sandpaper-like bumps allow an even better grip on their slippery meals. The nest is a huge mass of sticks that they add to each year, built on top of trees, snags, poles, or just about anything near water, including manmade objects such as power poles. Like the bald eagle, whose population decreased due to pesticide use, the osprey has been making a nice comeback since the ban of DDT.

Osprey bringing fish to its young.

HABITAT near water and coastlines

RANGE coastal and western U.S. into Canada and Alaska; winters in some southern coastal areas of U.S. and farther south

ORDER Falconiformes: the raptors

YOUNG semialtricial, asynchronous

CLUTCH SIZE 2–4

AMERICAN COOT ⚔ *FULICA AMERICANA*

THE RODNEY DANGERFIELD OF BIRDS?

Found just about everywhere in North America, these guys are very common members of the rail family. They look like ducks but aren't, they nest like grebes but aren't, they're all black like blackbirds but aren't… They're coots. Their lobed (not webbed) feet have flaps of skin between the toes. The adult's beak is all white and the eyes are a beautiful red. Born so ugly they are cute, these precocial chicks will swim around pecking food off the surface of the water.

HABITAT wetlands, both salt and fresh water; nest over water on piled-up vegetation

RANGE throughout North America

ORDER Gruiformes: the cranes, rails, and coots

YOUNG subprecocial

CLUTCH SIZE 2–22 (will add to other birds' nests)

American coot.

SANDHILL CRANE ⋈ *GRUS CANADENSIS*

MAGICAL MUSICIANS.

We have two species of cranes in the U.S.: the sandhill and the endangered whooping crane. Sandhills make my favorite bird call, which ranks right up there with the wolf howl as the two sounds reminding me most of wilderness America. The sandhill's call can be heard over a mile away, which is attributed to its unusual windpipe. This trachea is elongated and looped, much like a trumpet, giving this bird a truly musical tone. The whooping crane has an even longer trachea, with two loops.

Sandhill crane chick.

HABITAT tundra, marshes, grasslands, dry fields, and roosts in water at night; nest built on dry land or constructed of floating vegetation over water

RANGE winters in central California and southern states from Arizona to Florida; breeds in northern North America

ORDER Gruiformes: the cranes, rails, and coots

YOUNG subprecocial

CLUTCH SIZE 2

AMERICAN GOLDEN-PLOVER ⪦ *PLUVIALIS DOMINICA*
SNOWY PLOVER ⪦ *CHARADRIUS ALEXANDRINUS*
KILLDEER ⪦ *CHARADRIUS VOCIFERUS*

"CRYING WOLF" WITH A BROKEN WING.

Snowy plover.

Plovers will make a scrape in the ground and lay four pebble-like eggs camouflaged with speckles. The golden-plover, a long-distance migrator, will nest in the Arctic tundra and then fly to southern South America for the winter. Coastal-nesting snowy plovers will nest just above the high-tide line on the beach sand, leaving them vulnerable to predators and certain human activities; snowies have been declining due to nesting damage as beaches become more popular. Killdeer are among the most commonly enjoyed birds in urban areas.

Killdeer.

As with other plovers, when the killdeer settles in to incubate, it will lie motionless until a predator gets too close, whereupon the killdeer will limp off with the famous broken-wing trick, feigning injury to draw the danger away from the nest. This technique is very common among the ground-nesting birds. Killdeer are named for their call, which sounds like *kill-dee*.

HABITAT golden-plover: Arctic tundra and coastlines; snowy: saltwater habitats (beaches, dry mud, salt flats); killdeer: grassy fields, open areas, and shorelines; all three nest in a scrape on the ground

RANGE golden: nests in Arctic, winters in South America; snowy: coastal areas along U.S. west and Gulf coasts, some nest in salty areas of western U.S. and south to Texas; killdeer: throughout North America

ORDER Charadriiformes: the shorebirds

YOUNG semiprecocial

CLUTCH SIZE 4 for most plovers; 3 for snowy

AMERICAN AVOCET ⪥ *RECURVIROSTRA AMERICANA*
BLACK-NECKED STILT ⪥ *HIMANTOPUS MEXICANUS*

HIGH-WATER GALS AND GUYS.

Black-necked stilt.

These long-legged, ground-nesting shorebirds have given me many memorable experiences with baby birds. Their well-camouflaged eggs have greenish and blackish speckles that blend in with the marshy surroundings. At birth their beaks look pretty normal, but as the birds grow their bills also grow. The avocet's curves upward into a distinctive, upturned, long slender beak; the stilt's bill, on the other hand, just gets a lot longer. Both species have long legs, which is how the stilt got its name. Like many colonial nesters, these birds will protect their nest and young tirelessly, making the nesting area a very noisy, active place.

American avocet.

HABITAT wetlands—shallow ponds, marshes, lake shores, and coastal areas; nest in a scrape in the ground near water

RANGE American avocet: winters along coasts from California to Carolinas, breeds inland in western U.S.; black-necked stilt: same as American avocet but breeds throughout range

ORDER Charadriiformes: the shorebirds

YOUNG precocial

CLUTCH SIZE 4

SEMIPALMATED SANDPIPER ⊰ *CALIDRIS PUSILLA*

KALEIDOSCOPES OF FLIGHT.

These small sandpipers can fly long distances from their nesting grounds in the Arctic to winter in South America. My favorite time to watch sandpipers is during migration, when they congregate in large numbers. In flight, these huge flocks become a kaleidoscopic wonder, resembling an aerial school of fish. They all twist and turn at the same time, showing their pale bellies and then shifting, creating a flash of brown—truly an amazing sight.

HABITAT Alaska and Arctic in summer, migrating south along freshwater shorelines and mudflats; nest hidden in grass on ground

RANGE Alaska and Arctic for breeding and South America for winter

ORDER Charadriiformes: the shorebirds

YOUNG precocial

CLUTCH SIZE 4

GLAUCOUS GULL ⤲ *LARUS HYPERBOREUS*
CALIFORNIA GULL ⤲ *LARUS CALIFORNICUS*
MEW GULL ⤲ *LARUS CANUS*

WE'RE NOT SEAGULLS ... JUST GULLS!

Often considered pests because of their scavenging ways and association with dumps, gulls will feed on anything they deem worthy of swallowing. I once saw one swallow a sea star whole, and I have seen them caught on hooks after going for a fisherman's bait. Most gulls take three years to reach sexual maturity and adult

California gulls.

plumage coloration. For birdwatchers, juvenile gulls present some of the most difficult identification challenges. California gulls are honored by the State of Utah for an event in the mid-1800s: during a crop-ruining Mormon cricket infestation, the gulls saved the day by eating the insects. There is even a monument in their honor in the state capitol at Salt Lake City.

Mew gull.

HABITAT glaucous: mostly coastlines, nesting on ground and cliffs; California: coastlines and wetlands, nesting on ground in colonies; mew: coastlines and wetlands, nesting near freshwater on rocks, hummocks, or trees
RANGE glaucous: winters along both coasts from California to Alaska and Carolinas northward, breeds throughout the coastal Arctic; California: winters along U.S. west coast, nests in

northwestern U.S. and Canada; mew: winters along west coast of
North America, nests in western Canada and Alaska

ORDER Charadriiformes: the shorebirds

YOUNG semiprecocial

CLUTCH SIZE 2–3

ARCTIC TERN ☌ *STERNA PARADISAEA*
LEAST TERN ☌ *STERNA ANTILLARUM*
WHITE TERN ☌ *GYGIS ALBA*

AT HOME IN A SCRAPE OR A DENT.

"Long-distance flier" is an understatement for the Arctic tern. After
nesting in the Arctic during our summer, they fly an amazing 11,000
miles to the Antarctic during our winter—thus enjoying the long days
of both northern- and southern-hemisphere summers. Talk about
migration: these terns fly halfway around the world every six months
for an annual distance of 22,000 miles! Formerly named "fairy tern,"
the white tern's color contrasts nicely with its black eyes and bill, and
when hovering they do resemble fairies. They will nest in nothing
more than a natural dent on a log or branch, where they will lay a single precariously balanced egg. North America's smallest tern, the

endangered least tern, digs a cup-shaped nest in the ground. Terns eat fish and will carry them back to their young, who swallow them whole. Dinner could be as big as the baby that swallows it.

Least terns in their ground nest.

HABITAT Arctic tern: wetlands and coastal areas; white tern: coastlines and shorelines; least tern: beaches and sandbars; nest in a scrape on the ground (Arctic and least terns) or a dent in a branch or log (white terns)

RANGE Arctic tern: nest throughout the Arctic and winter in the Antarctic; white tern: favor Hawaii and the tropical to subtropical areas of the Pacific, Indian, and south Atlantic Oceans; least tern: most U.S. coastlines, with some scattered populations inland

ORDER Charadriiformes: the shorebirds

YOUNG semiprecocial

CLUTCH SIZE 1–3

BARN OWL ⊰ *TYTO ALBA*
GREAT HORNED OWL ⊰ *BUBO VIRGINIANUS*
NORTHERN SPOTTED OWL ⊰ *STRIX OCCIDENTALIS*

VALENTINE FACES AND SKUNK HUNTERS.

The barn owl's unique heart-shaped facial disk is evident in young fledglings. These common owls often take shelter and even nest in barns (hence the name). Great horned owls, with their strong talons and sharp beaks, are among the fiercest predators in the bird world.

They will even dine on a skunk, as they lack a sense of smell. They are fiercely protective of their nests; one summer while I worked at a peregrine falcon hack site, owls killed some of our fledgling peregrines. The northern spotted owl has been a "spokesman" for old-growth forests, which serve as their main habitat. They aren't in the news as often today, but thankfully they still reside in the forests of the West. Their dark eyes and spotted brown-and-white bodies provide great camouflage amid the shadows and sunlight streaming onto the forest floor.

HABITAT barn owl: grassland, woodland, meadow, wetland edges, and deserts, nesting in dark cavities in buildings, trees, cliffs; great horned: city to forest to desert, nesting in trees, cliffs, or on ground; northern spotted: wooded canyons, humid forests, nesting in cavities or on platforms of large trees

ABOVE: *Barn owl.* RIGHT: *Spotted owl.*

RANGE barn owl: throughout U.S. except northernmost states; great horned: throughout North America; northern spotted: the three coastal Northwestern states

ORDER Strigiformes: the owls

YOUNG semialtricial

CLUTCH SIZE barn owl 3–11, great horned 1–6, northern spotted 1–4

ANNA'S HUMMINGBIRD ⋈ *CALYPTE ANNA*

SINGLE MOMS.

One of sixteen nesting species of hummer in North America, only the Anna's winters primarily in the United States. The male Anna's is the only male hummer that routinely sings from a perch, and they protect their territory vigorously. Male hummingbirds will mate with many females, who are then solely responsible for the nesting duties and "child" rearing. Meanwhile the male continues to attract mates and defend his territory. These single moms often raise more than one brood per year.

HABITAT coastal lowlands, deserts, and mountains with mild climates; tiny cup nests made of spiderwebs and grasses

Anna's hummingbird.

RANGE western U.S. from Arizona to Canada

ORDER Apodiformes: the hummingbirds and swifts

YOUNG altricial

CLUTCH SIZE 2 (eggs the size of jelly beans)

NORTHERN FLICKER ⊰ *COLAPTES AURATUS*

DRUMMERS OF THE FOREST.

Northern flicker.

Flickers are the "anteaters" of the bird world. Although these woodpeckers will drill holes in trees for nesting, they primarily feed on the ground, digging and scratching for ants. Their long tongue has barbs on it to aid in ant-catching. Since they don't have very strong drilling beaks, they seek out softer wood and dead trees for hollowing their nest cavities. We have one that likes to drum on the side of our softwood house in spring, creating quite a knocking sound, but also damaging the siding. Woodpecker drumming is associated with breeding and the attracting of a mate.

HABITAT open woodlands, suburban areas with trees
RANGE throughout North America
ORDER Piciformes: the woodpeckers
YOUNG altricial
CLUTCH SIZE 5–8

GRAY FLYCATCHER ⊰ *EMPIDONAX WRIGHTII*
BLENDING INTO THE SAGEBRUSH.

A member of the *Empidonax* genus, which consists of eleven North American flycatchers so similar they are a challenge to identify. When a species looks like a dozen others, we rely on habits, range, voice, and habitat to identify them. One unique habit of the gray flycatcher is that it flicks its tail downward, whereas its look-alikes flick theirs upward. Their habitat of sage and juniper woodlands also helps define this bird. Flycatchers generally hunt from a perch, flying out to catch an insect in flight, returning to the perch, then repeating the process.

Gray flycatcher.

HABITAT dry areas of sagebrush, pine, or piñon-juniper forests; grassy cup nests

RANGE summer migrant in Great Basin, dry areas of western U.S.

ORDER Passeriformes: the perching birds

YOUNG altricial

CLUTCH SIZE 3–4

COMMON RAVEN ⊰ *CORVUS CORAX*

OVERSIZED MISCHIEF-MAKERS.

America's largest songbird and passerine resembles its smaller cousins, the crows. Revered and often portrayed as tricksters in Native American folklore, they are known to harass other animals and have been observed pulling on their tails. Ravens and crows are thought to be very intelligent birds.

HABITAT varied, including deserts, mountains, and coastal areas; nest of sticks on cliffs

RANGE western and northern North America

ORDER Passeriformes: the perching birds

YOUNG altricial

CLUTCH SIZE 3–7

Common raven.

CLIFF SWALLOW ⚮ *PETROCHELIDON PYRRHONOTA*

ARCHITECTS WITH MUD.

"The swallows have returned to San Juan Capistrano"—we hear this every March 19, and like clockwork, their return is news. Historically, cliff swallows nested on the sides of cliffs, hence the name. With so many manmade vertical objects around today, like the San Juan Capistrano mission, we find them nesting on buildings and under bridges too. The nest is an igloo-shaped mud contraption, made one beakful at a time. Watching these swallows gathering mud, you can appreciate their construction abilities.

HABITAT rural areas with bridges, open country, and cliffs for nesting; colonial nesters with gourd-shaped nests of mud
RANGE summers throughout North America except extreme Southeast, flies south for winter
ORDER Passeriformes: the perching birds
YOUNG altricial
CLUTCH SIZE 4–5

CANYON WREN ◁ *CATHERPES MEXICANUS*
MELODIES FROM THE CANYONS.

A sweet songster, the canyon wren brings music to some remote rocky areas and canyons. If a canyon wren sings and nobody is there to here it, does it make a sound? Of course it does! Wrens are secretive "Little Brown Jobbers" (LBJs), more often heard than seen. The acronym LBJ is often playfully used for unidentifiable small brown birds.

HABITAT canyons, rocky areas, and cliffs; cup nests on ledges in caverns and rock crevices
RANGE Texas to Montana and westward
ORDER Passeriformes: the perching birds

Canyon wrens.

YOUNG altricial

CLUTCH SIZE 4–7

MOUNTAIN BLUEBIRD *SIALIA CURRUCOIDES*

THESE BLUE SINGERS DON'T SING THE BLUES.

Bluebirds are backyard favorites for many people in North America. The three species include Eastern, Western, and Mountain blue-

Mountain bluebirds.

birds, and they are secondary cavity nesters—they will nest in manmade nest boxes, too. This gives us a great way to enjoy nesting birds up close. Some bluebird fanatics actually put up dozens of boxes that they maintain over the nesting season.

HABITAT open areas like meadows, often above 5,000-foot elevation

RANGE western North America

ORDER Passeriformes: the perching birds

YOUNG altricial

CLUTCH SIZE 4–7

AMERICAN ROBIN *TURDUS MIGRATORIUS*

WORM CATCHER.

The widespread "robin redbreast" is found throughout the United States. They build the typical cup-shaped nest with mud and grasses and fill it with bluish eggs. The American robin feeds on worms in grassy areas, and as they feed they will stop, cock their heads to the side, and look down for the next worm. Keeping your lawns and yards healthy and free of pesticides is important for maintaining healthy robins and other bird species in your yard.

HABITAT yardbirds, using lawns, meadows, shrubs, and trees; cup nests made of mud and grasses

RANGE throughout North America

ORDER Passeriformes: the perching birds

YOUNG altricial

CLUTCH SIZE 3–4

American robins.

CALIFORNIA TOWHEE ❧ *PIPILO CRISSALIS*

TERRITORIAL HOMEBODIES.

This nest was in my wife's garden one spring, right outside my office window. Watching the parents bring food to their three young made it tough to concentrate on my writing, so I grabbed my camera instead. Luckily for me they re-nested and actually raised two sets of young, back to back. Formerly named brown towhee, the California towhee and canyon towhee have been split into two distinct species.

California towhees.

HABITAT oak woodlands, chaparral, parks, and gardens; open cup nests of weeds, grass, and fur

RANGE western Oregon to Baja California, Mexico

ORDER Passeriformes: the perching birds

YOUNG altrical

CLUTCH SIZE 3–4

RED CROSSBILL ⇥ *LOXIA CURVIROSTRA*

WANDERING CONE-CRACKERS.

One of the most interesting beaks in the bird world belongs to the crossbills. Their top mandible actually crosses over the lower mandible, hence the name. They will insert this beak into a pine cone, then open wide to spread the scales on the cones so they can

Red crossbills.

remove the seeds with their tongues. Crossbills are very nomadic and will go where the conifer cones offer lots of seeds to eat. North America also has a white-winged crossbill.

HABITAT coniferous woods; open cup nest of twigs, grass, and fur
RANGE Rocky Mountains, Pacific Northwest, Canada, and
northeastern U.S., where cone-bearing trees occur
ORDER Passeriformes: the perching birds
YOUNG altrical
CLUTCH SIZE 3–5

SUGGESTED READING

Baicich, Paul J. *A Guide to the Nests, Eggs, and Nestlings of North American Birds.* San Diego, CA: Academic Press, 1997.

Broyles, Bill. *Desert Babies.* Tucson, AZ: Rio Nuevo Publishers, 2005.

Harrison, Hal H. *A Field Guide to Western Birds' Nests.* Boston, MA: Houghton Mifflin, 2001.

Kaufman, Kenn. *Lives of North American Birds.* Boston, MA: Houghton Mifflin, 1996.

Kaufman, Lynn Hassler. *Gambel's Quail.* Tucson, AZ: Rio Nuevo Publishers, 2004.

——. *Roadrunners.* Tucson, AZ: Rio Nuevo Publishers, 2004.

National Geographic Field Guide to the Birds of North America. Washington, D.C.: National Geographic, 1999.

Sibley, David Allen. *The Sibley Guide to Bird Life and Behavior.* Westminster, MD: Alfred A. Knopf, 2001.

Stokes, Donald, and Lillian Stokes. *Stokes Guide to Bird Behavior* (Vols. 1, 2, 3). London: Little, Brown and Co., 1979, 1983, 1983.

INDEX